SOVIE*trek*

E*trek*

A Journey by Bicycle across Russia

Written and photographed by
DAN BUETTNER

LERNER PUBLICATIONS COMPANY/MINNEAPOLIS

For Spanky

*Additional photographs courtesy of: p. 38, Mansell Collection; p. 56, © Galem Rowell /
Peter Arnold; p. 70, Bryan Liedahl. All maps by Laura Westlund.*

Words in **bold type** are listed in a glossary that begins on
page 101.

LIBRARY OF CONGRESS CATALOGING-IN-PUBLICATION DATA

Buettner, Dan.
   Sovietrek: a journey by bicycle across Russia / written
   and photographed by Dan Buettner.
   p. cm.
   Includes index,
   ISBN 0-8225-2950-5 (lib. bdg.)
   1. Russia, Description and travel—Juvenile literature.
2. Buettner, Dan—Journeys—Russia, Juvenile literature.
[1. Russia, Description and travel.] I. Title.
DK510.29.B84 1994
947.086—dc20   94-5449
                                                            CIP
                                                            AC

Manufactured in the United States of America
1 2 3 4 5 6 I/JR 99 98 97 96 95 94

CONTENTS

A Note from the Author

Our journey across southern Russia began in June of 1990, the last full year the **Soviet Union** was in existence. For 40 years before that time, the Soviet Union was America's military opponent, and in some ways, its enemy.

But things in the Soviet Union were changing, and Soviet leaders were making great efforts to improve relations with the United States. I thought a trip by a team of two Americans and two Soviets—cycling on

mountain bikes across the rough landscape of southern Russia—would symbolize cooperation between our two nations.

For this journey, which we called Sovietrek, we'd put together a perfect team. My brother Steve had joined me in 1986 on a 15,536-mile bike ride from North America to the tip of South America. He's a crack bicycle mechanic and a good friend. Volodya is a schoolteacher from Novosibirsk, a major city in **Siberia**—a huge section of eastern Russia. He and I had met in 1989 and had spent a year planning Sovietrek.

During Sovietrek, Steve Buettner struggled to propel his bike through the mud of Siberia, a vast region of eastern Russia.

The four members of Sovietrek were Alexander Rozumenko *(above left)*, **Steve Buettner** *(above center)*, **Volodya Kovalenko** *(above right)*, **and** Dan Buettner *(below)*.

Volodya had recruited Alexander, a biologist who had skied to the North Pole and who had lived in Antarctica for 14 months. In addition to being a tough, experienced explorer, Alexander had medical training and would serve as our doctor. Alexander and Volodya spoke fluent Russian, and their language skills would help us a lot on our trek.

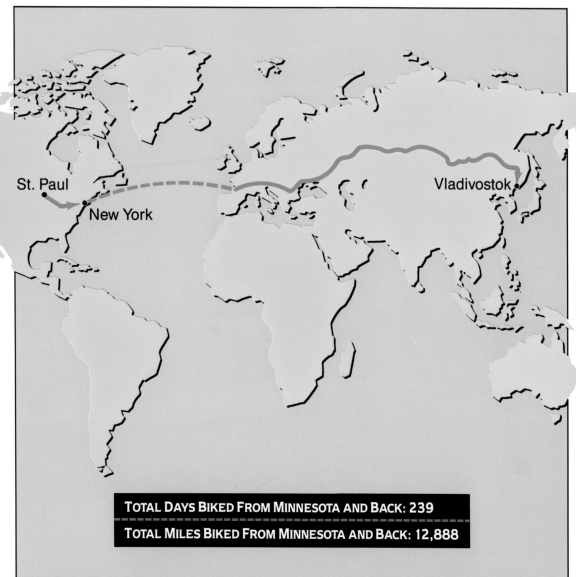

St. Paul

New York

Vladivostok

TOTAL DAYS BIKED FROM MINNESOTA AND BACK: 239

TOTAL MILES BIKED FROM MINNESOTA AND BACK: 12,888

The four members of Sovietrek—Dan and Steve Buettner, Volodya Kovalenko, and Alexander Rozumenko—left St. Paul, Minnesota, on April 1, 1990. They pedaled eastward from Minnesota to New York, where they boarded a flight to Europe. After the plane landed in France on April 20, the group cycled through France, Italy, Serbia (then part of Yugoslavia), and Romania before reaching the border of the Soviet Union on June 4, 1990.

The foursome spent the next 124 days biking eastward through grasslands, mountains, and mud to get to Vladivostok, a port on the Pacific Ocean. From Vladivostok, team members flew via Moscow, the Russian capital, to Los Angeles, California, where they again unpacked their bikes to cycle 2,200 miles back to St. Paul. The journey took 239 days. The total distance from beginning to end was 12,888. The Soviet leg of the trek covered 7,353 miles.

Steve and I worked for 18 months to raise the $50,000 needed for expenses. We wrote to more than 800 U.S. companies to ask for sponsorship. Just a handful replied, and most of the time they offered only equipment. Then one day I got an appointment with a manager at 3M, a large corporation headquartered in my home state of Minnesota. 3M makes Scotchlite, a reflective material that is applied directly to clothing.

I knew from previous experience that traffic is one of the greatest dangers faced on a long bike trek. I figured that by wearing Scotchlite material we'd be more visible on the road. I tried to convince the 3M manager that if 3M's product could help keep us safe as we pedaled across Russia, the company could convince kids to wear Scotchlite to travel around the block. It worked!

While Steve and I raised money, Volodya and Alexander tried to get us visas (official travel papers). The Soviet Union had been closed to most foreigners for more than 70 years. Few Americans had ever gotten the kind of visas we were asking for. We wanted to bike on our own schedule, wherever we wanted, from one end of the country to the other.

Volodya spent weeks in the capital city of Moscow walking from agency to agency, pleading our case. He wrote

At night, Scotchlite reflective material made the bikers easier to see on the road.

hundreds of letters. His breakthrough came when he contacted Sputnik, the Soviet Union's youth travel organization. Sputnik believed our bike trek would show that the Soviet Union was opening up to the outside world. The organization used its high-level government contacts to get our visas.

Our final hurdle lay in planning the actual route. We knew that we wanted to bicycle from west to east across southern Russia—a distance of about 7,400 miles. However, we also knew that Soviet-made maps of Russia were famous for being wrong. The government had made the maps inaccurate on purpose so that they might fool the Soviet Union's enemies.

Dan, Steve, and Alexander studied one of several large maps to plan Sovietrek's route through southern Russia.

For help on finding accurate maps, I talked to a geography professor at the University of Minnesota. He told me about some little-known maps published by the U.S. State Department. Called Operational Navigation Charts (ONCs), these maps are used mainly by military pilots and show everything from tank factories to telephone poles. Most important for us, though, they also show roads.

I wrote to the address in Washington, D.C., that the professor had given me, enclosed a check, and requested the map I would need to cross the Soviet Union. A few weeks later, 11 maps arrived. When I placed them end to end, they stretched across my living room and dining room and into my kitchen! Sovietrek would be one long journey, but what an adventure!

INTRODUCTION

More than twice as big as the United States, the Soviet Union spanned 13 time zones and occupied about one-sixth of the earth's surface. In 1990 the Soviet Union was made up of 15 member-republics.

The largest republic was Russia, which covers huge sections of Europe and Asia. The low Ural Mountains separate **European Russia** from **Asian Russia.** Dominating the Asian part of Russia is Siberia, a vast region of about five million square miles.

The route of Sovietrek would take us through endless grasslands, called **steppes,** over the Ural Mountains, and across the southern part of the Western Siberian Plain. Continuing southeastward, we'd bike across the Central Siberian Plateau until we'd hit the Yablonovy Mountains that border Mongolia.

Wildflowers thrive on the Russian steppes (grasslands).

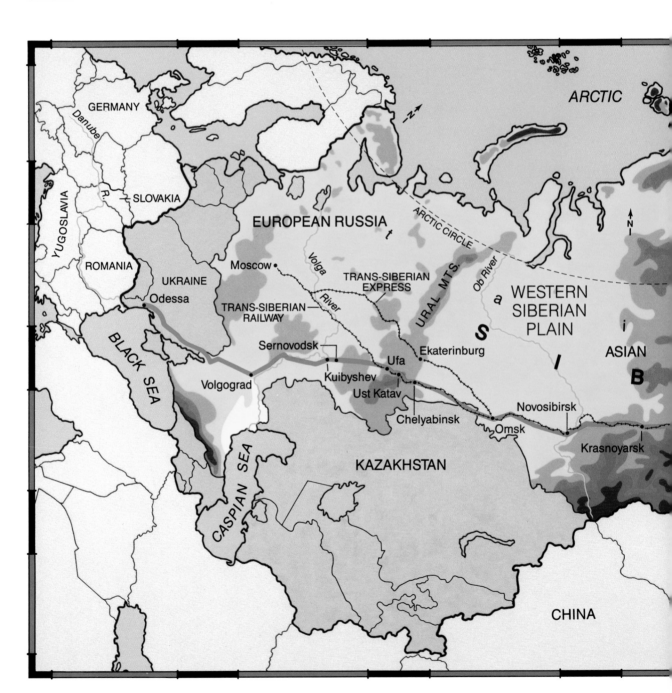

TOTAL DAYS BIKED IN THE SOVIET UNION: 124

TOTAL MILES BIKED IN THE SOVIET UNION: 7,353

We'd then reach an 800-mile bog and end the trek in Vladivostok. This large port on the Pacific Ocean is closer to Tokyo, Japan, than it is to Moscow!

Sovietrek would take us through large cities and into small villages. We'd pedal along some good roads as well as along many dirt tracks. We might even have to travel by river if the roads were too hard to bike.

We'd be able to see what life was like in rural Russia, particularly in Siberia. Although this region has long been home to Asian ethnic groups, such as the Buryat and the Yakut, most of the people who live in Siberia are Russian.

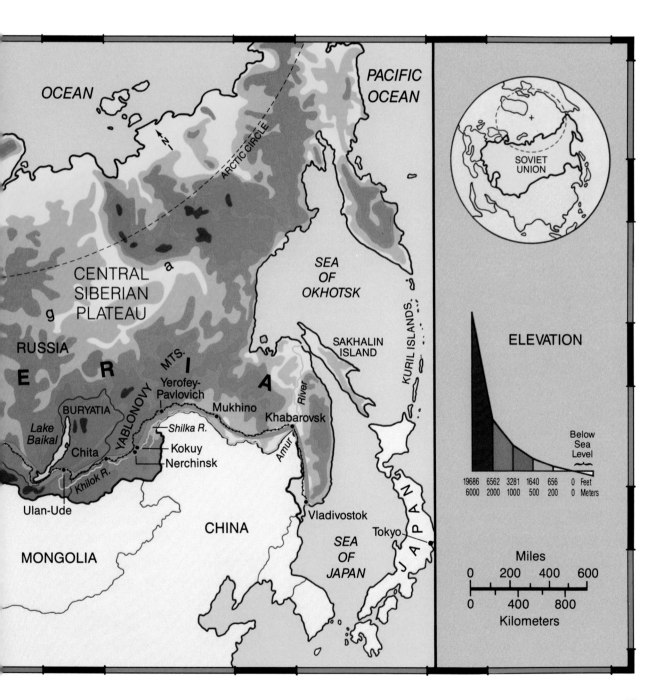

15

Soldiers applaud passing troops during a military parade in Volgograd, a large city in European Russia.

Our visas gave us official permission to enter the Soviet Union in June. Within the Siberian steppes, the average temperature in July—the hottest time of the year—was only 64° F. To avoid the chilly Siberian autumn, we'd need to finish Sovietrek by late September or early October. That meant we had to average more than 60 miles a day to make 7,400 miles in 120 days.

Like most Americans, I had only a vague idea of the Soviet Union. Whenever I tried to form a picture in my mind, it always appeared in black and white—like an old TV program. My mind's eye saw gray buildings, gray cars, and people in gray clothes who frowned a lot. I associated the Soviet Union with "the enemy." I wondered if the people there would see me as their enemy, too. I didn't know if I should be scared or just curious. I didn't know, but I wanted to find out. And what I found out surprised me.

16

Young girls *(above left)* play with their cat in west central Russia, and a lumberjack *(above right)* chops wood in Siberia. High-rise apartment buildings *(right)* dominate the city of Kokuy in eastern Siberia.

OFF TO A WET START

To reach Russia, we biked through several countries in eastern Europe, which in 1990 bordered the western Soviet Union. We entered Russia from Ukraine—then still a Soviet republic—which shares a frontier with Romania, Hungary, Slovakia, and Poland. Ukraine, which means "borderland" in the Russian language, sits between the thick forests of European Russia and the open steppes of Asian Russia.

Head down, I pedaled hard into a strong wind. Under my bicycle wheels, the road darted out in front of me and disappeared at a point on the horizon. On either side, wheat fields spread so far in the distance that they vanished with the curve of the earth. "Borderland?" I asked myself. "What borders?"

Volodya, Alexander, and Steve rode up ahead. Their 30-pound mountain bikes were loaded with another 70 pounds of equipment. Each of us was weighed down with four saddlebags, called **panniers.** They carried tents, sleeping bags, clothes, tools, spare parts, tire-patching kits, cameras, books, diaries, tape players, radios, passports, visas, money, food, and water. Our team looked like a small herd of rolling pack mules.

From April to June 1990, the team biked through central Europe to reach the Soviet Union. Here, Steve and Alexander cycle along a paved road that follows the course of Europe's Danube River.

From the Ukrainian border we pedaled east to the large Russian city of Volgograd. Here, we turned north and followed the Volga River, Russia's main waterway, to the city of Kuibyshev. It was mid-June, and we had warm, summerlike temperatures. The day we left Kuibyshev and pedaled eastward, however, all that changed.

It rained. Actually it poured. We pedaled all day long, and by sundown we were still looking for a place to stay. We were tired and wet. My rear wheel had sprayed a strip of mud up my back. There was even dirt in my underwear.

All day we'd seen endless fields that stretched to the horizon. So far, I thought, bicycling across Russia wasn't much different from bicycling across the Great Plains of North Dakota.

Next to me I saw a large truck. *"Zdrazstzuite!"* A friendly voice came through the rain. The truck's driver was poking his head out the window and saying hello.

"Zdrazstzuite!" I shouted back over the roar of his engine.

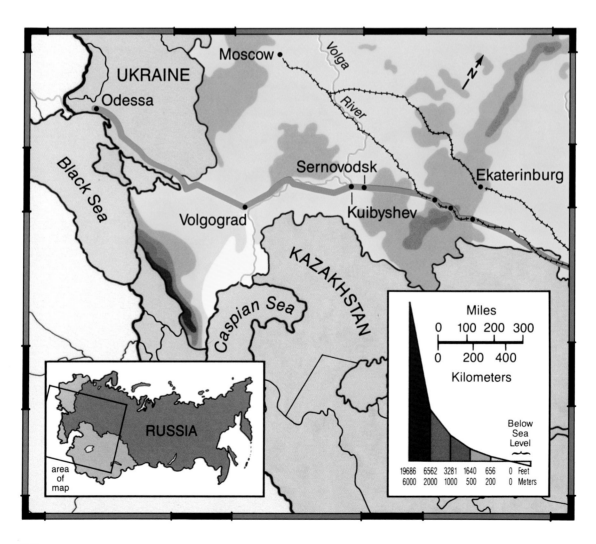

A farmer and his son *(above)* transport food for their livestock along the Volga River. Near the border between Russia and Ukraine, a rainbow *(right)* arches over a highway.

"Otkuda?" he said, asking me where I was from.

"America!" I answered.

The truck screeched to a halt. Vladimir, the heavy-set driver, hurried out. He grabbed my hand and shook it hard. Vladimir, like most people in this region, had never met an American.

He immediately flooded me with questions that I didn't understand. So I waited for Volodya and Alexander to catch up.

Vladimir invited us to his home in the nearby village of Sernovodsk, where he lived with his wife, Natasha, and his three children. Russian homes are not big. In

Vladimir's case, two bedrooms, a living room, and a kitchen housed the entire family. The bathroom was an outhouse at the end of a large garden, which was planted with vegetables and herbs. A cow, a dozen chickens, and a gaggle of geese shared Vladimir's fenced-in yard.

Steve, Alexander, Volodya, and I stood inside the house's doorway dripping rainwater on the floor. Vladimir brought us towels and dry clothes. Natasha, who had just come from her job as a teacher, washed our muddy clothes by boiling them in a huge pot on the kitchen stove. Then she began to prepare our dinner.

Meanwhile, Vladimir had found a comfortable seat on the couch and had unfolded a map of Russia. He wanted to know how we planned to cross his country. Alexander showed him by tracing his finger from Sernovodsk, to the Ural Mountains, then all the way across Siberia to Vladivostok.

Vladimir pointed to eastern Siberia and shook his head. *"Nevozmozhni,"* he said. "Impossible. You can't bicycle there; no roads. Just 800 miles of swamp and bog." We didn't answer, but our plans were set. We'd remember Vladimir's remarks in the grueling days ahead.

At dinner, Natasha served cucumbers, a beef and cabbage soup called *borscht,* blood sausage, and two loaves of heavy brown bread. Before we began

YOU CAN'T BICYCLE THERE; NO ROADS. JUST 800 MILES OF SWAMP AND BOG.

to eat, Vladimir poured us all a small glass of vodka. He bowed his head and proposed a toast. "In my country, we judge a man by how well he treats his guests," he said. Then looking at us he added, "You are always welcome in my home."

Before I left America, I had read that there were food shortages in the Soviet Union and that people had to stand in long lines for food. I asked Vladimir if that were true.

"Yes and no," he replied. "For things like sugar, canned fish, and vodka, we must stand in long lines and even then we can only buy small amounts. But people like us who live in small villages...we grow most of our food in our yards."

Many rural homes in Russia don't have indoor plumbing, so family members draw water from a backyard well for washing and cooking. Well-kept gardens provide much of the family's food.

Russians often wait in long lines to buy food. There's even a delay at the McDonald's "fast-food" restaurant in Moscow, the capital city of Russia.

"You mean everything we ate for dinner came from your backyard?"

"Of course. Everything except the bread and the vodka."

I envied the constant supply of fresh food. Most Americans never eat an entire meal grown a few feet from their dinner tables.

The conversation went on for several hours before we got ready for bed. When I noticed that Vladimir was making his children sleep on the floor so that we could sleep in their beds, I began to protest. Alexander grabbed my arm firmly and said, "You must accept this hospitality, Dan. It's our custom."

In bed I lay awake listening to the pitter-patter of rain on the roof and the sounds of Natasha in the kitchen. I remembered that if it hadn't been for Vladimir's and Natasha's kindness, we would be wet, cold, hungry, and sleeping outside.

Then I asked Alexander why Natasha was still up. "Because she is preparing a very special breakfast for us," he replied from the bed next to mine.

We awoke at sunrise and started the day, as usual, by making small repairs to our bikes and packing our gear. At 8:00 A.M., Natasha called us to the table and proudly presented us with the meal she had stayed up late to prepare. Steve and I looked in our bowls to find cold beef in a clear jelly with big chunks of fat—a dish called *studen.* For Volodya and Alexander, this was a gourmet meal. But my brother and I, not being used to this kind of food, had to force down each bite. In a way, studen was one of the worst meals I'd ever eaten. But the warmth with which Natasha served it made it one of the best, too.

RECIPE

Studen, or meat molded in a clear jelly made from meat stock, takes a long time to prepare. The name studen comes from an old Russian word that means "chilled," and cooks insist the dish must be very cold before being taken out of the mold and put on a platter. Here's one of several ways to make studen.

4½ quarts cold water
2½ pounds calf's or pig's feet
1 pound beef chuck, plus bone
1 pound chicken necks, skin removed
1 medium onion
1 medium carrot

8 black peppercorns
1 generous tablespoon salt
2 bay leaves
1 whole head of garlic
2 teaspoons salt
½ teaspoon black pepper

In a large pot, heat the water until warm and then add the calf's or pig's feet, the beef chuck, and the chicken necks. Bring the water to a boil and then immediately reduce to a simmer. Skim off the foam as it rises to the surface. When the foam has stopped rising, add the onion, carrot, peppercorns, and one tablespoon of salt. Partially cover the pot and gently simmer the broth until it thickens and has reduced by about one-half. Add the bay leaves after the broth has been simmering for five hours.

After simmering for one more hour, strain the liquid through cheesecloth into a clean pot. There should be about two quarts. Discard the carrot and onion. Remove the meat from the chicken necks and shred it and the beef chuck. Peel the garlic cloves and put them through a garlic press. Mix the garlic, salt, and pepper with the shredded meat.

Brush four one-quart molds lightly with vegetable oil. Pour enough broth in each mold to cover the bottom generously and chill until the broth has formed a clear jelly. Place a layer of meat on the jelly and cover with the remaining broth. Chill the molds for eight hours. To unmold, run a knife around the edges of the jelly to loosen and invert the mold over a plate. Serve well chilled with spicy mustard. Makes 12 to 16 servings.

At the start of Sovietrek, the bikes were loaded with spare tires and other equipment.

In Sernovodsk, the village where Vladimir and Natasha lived, a woman washed clothes in a branch of the Volga River.

AN UPHILL BATTLE

After pedaling away from Vladimir's house in Serno-vodsk, we saw more wheat fields and flat plains. Only after the industrial city of Ufa did our road slope up toward the rolling hills and misty pine forests of the Ural Mountains.

The Urals run the length of Russia like a low picket fence. They separate European Russia in the west from Siberia in the east. Despite their geographic importance, the Ural Mountains are not high. They stand

lower than most mountain ranges in the United States. But they looked big to us.

As we steadily pedaled uphill, Alexander suddenly cried, "Wait!" Steve, Volodya, and I squeezed our brakes and turned our bikes around. When we neared Alexander, he stood next to his crippled bike. His pedal had ripped off with the force of pedaling uphill and was now completely useless. "It looks like I'm not going anywhere," he said.

Team members traveled along a straight, paved road through the Ural Mountains, a low range that divides European Russia in the west from Asian Russia in the east. The pressure of cycling uphill broke Alexander's pedal arm, the part that links the pedal to the bike's chain wheel. He left the trek temporarily to get it fixed.

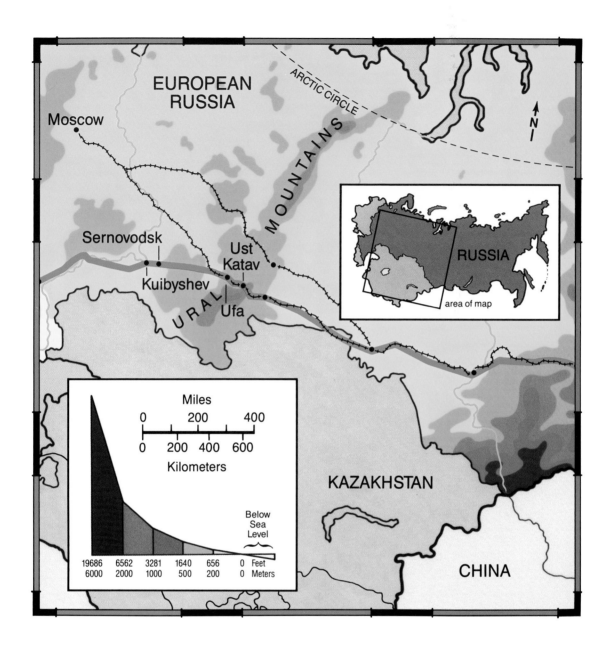

It looked bad. Alexander couldn't pedal his bike with only one pedal, we had no spare, and the next place up ahead to buy a new pedal was in Japan, 6,600 miles away! Worse, we were 100 miles from the next town.

"I'll have to turn back to Ufa and try to call some friends of mine in Moscow for help," said Alexander sadly. "You guys go on ahead, I will catch up—I hope." With no other logical choice, we left Alexander behind.

I felt bad to leave him. In a short time, he'd become an important part of our team. He often made a special effort to cycle with Steve and me so he could explain unfamiliar things to us. He took time to teach us the Cyrillic alpha-

A sign in Cyrillic, the Russian alphabet, announces that this building is a *stolovaya*, or cafeteria.

bet, in which the Russian language is written, so that we could sound out Russian road signs. He'd warn us well ahead of time if we needed to make a turn.

Steve, Volodya, and I cycled deeper into the Ural Mountains. The forests got thicker and the villages more rustic. At the top of hills, roadside vendors offered us jars of blueberries, pickles, and honey—each for what amounted to about a dime.

Roadside vendors offered the team a jar of blueberries for sale. The man holds a Sovietrek key ring that Dan gave him.

BALANCING STYLES

During the first part of the trip, Alexander and Dan didn't get along very well. Alexander was a slow, steady cyclist who could pedal for hours at a time. Dan, on the other hand, was faster but took many breaks. The difference in the two cycling styles often caused Alexander to become separated from the rest of the group. In Europe, for example, the team lost him for three days. By the time they'd reached the Ural Mountains, though, Alexander and Dan had found a balance between their biking styles and had started to become close friends.

In the woods next to the road, occasionally we'd meet people picking wild mushrooms, or *gribi*. An important food source, gribi were also the excuse for a popular family outing—gribi hunting.

At sunset, we turned off the highway into the village of Ust Katav. Smoke curled from the chimneys of wooden homes. In the yards, cows grazed, pigs wallowed in mud, and chickens pecked at the ground.

Ox-drawn carts rumbled down dirt streets. Some of the carts carried big loads of hay; others held 10-gallon milk cans. Women lined up with buckets at the village well. It was a scene out of the past, as if 100 years of changes hadn't happened here.

Along the road, we stopped to talk to a *babushka* (a Russian word that literally means "grandmother") who was bending over a row of cabbages in her garden. *"Izvinite!"* "Excuse me," Volodya called from out-

A family displays its harvest of wild mushrooms, called *gribi*.

An elderly Russian woman, or *babushka,* returns from her daily trip to get water from a community well.

In the foothills of the Ural Mountains, a group of boys *(left)* and their sister play on a hay wagon outside their log home. Inside, the little girl visits with her grandmother *(above)* in the kitchen.

side the fence. "We are an American-Soviet team bicycling across Russia. Can you suggest a place for us to sleep tonight?"

"Volodya, shouldn't we find dinner first?" I whispered. It was 10:00 P.M., and we hadn't eaten since lunch.

"Don't worry, Dan," Volodya replied. "If this woman invites us into her house she will give us food....It's a Russian custom."

The elderly woman, whose name was Elena, did invite us to stay the night. We leaned our bikes against her house, and she led us into her kitchen. Like most older Russian women, Elena wore a scarf over her head, a simple dress, and black rubber boots. She had large hands that were roughened from years of hard work.

Elena opened a trap door in the kitchen floor and climbed down into an earthen cellar. She came up with a pan full of potatoes, jars of pickled mushrooms, and jam. On a wood-burning stove, she boiled the potatoes and dropped six eggs into a pan of sputtering grease. Our entire dinner, except for the tea, came from Elena's backyard. We ate our fill as Volodya spoke Russian with Elena and her husband, Vasily.

"Good news," said Volodya, turning to Steve and me. "Vasily says tonight is Saturday—**banya** night. You will experience a great Russian tradition." And, as I was about to discover, I would also experience a great deal of pain.

In the backyard, smoke billowed from the chimney of a wooden bathhouse. As tradition dictated, Steve, Volodya, Vasily, and I stripped naked and stepped inside. The heat was incredible. A fire under the building heated a pile of rocks and a tank of water in the corner.

As the team cycled through rural areas, Volodya often stopped to get directions from local residents.

A man stokes the fire under his *banya*, or Russian bathhouse, in the village of Ust Katav.

Benches ran along the cedar plank walls. Basins, scrub brushes, soap, and bunches of birch branches littered the floor. I looked at a thermometer on the wall. It read 92° C—equal to 198° F, I calculated. Just 14 degrees short of boiling!

Water that Vasily scooped from a tank hissed as it hit the rocks. A cloud of steam rose up. The air grew thick, and breathing it was like breathing hot liquid. My head felt like it was in a pressure cooker. Dizzy, both Steve and I sat down.

Vasily and Volodya held their stomachs as they laughed at us. They were used to banyas.

"The best is yet to come," said Vasily as he

MY HEAD FELT LIKE IT WAS IN A PRESSURE COOKER.

began to scrub his body. "Next I will give you a Russian massage."

Steve went first. He lay belly-down on one of the benches. Vasily dipped a bunch of birch branches into a pail of pine-scented water and lifted them into the air. *Snap,* the branches came down on Steve's back. "Ahhh!" he cried in pain.

Vasily proceeded to whip my brother's back until it glowed bright red. "See," he said, "doesn't that feel good?" When Steve could take no more pain, he got up and ran out. Then Vasily turned to me.

The thrashing just tingled at first, then it stung. After a few minutes, those birch branches felt like razor blades on my back. Soon I, too, dashed out of the banya in pain.

The pain was gone by the time I dried off and dressed. In fact, I felt completely relaxed. Together, Steve and I walked briskly toward the house.

"Do you feel as good as I do?" I asked him on the way.

"I feel great!" he said energetically. "After that banya I could bicycle another hundred miles."

33

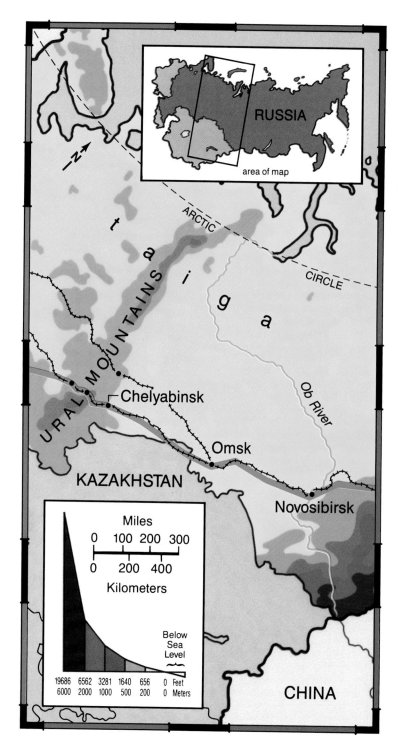

The horseflies that attacked the team were as big as a thumbnail.

thumbnail. They'd fly behind us until we stopped, and then they'd attack. When they bit, they drew blood. As Steve, Volodya, and I cycled this road, we couldn't help worrying about Alexander and wondering how he would make it alone. The three of us at least had one another to depend on.

The dirt road took us first to Chelyabinsk, one of the world's most polluted cities. We saw factory smokestacks belching out black smoke. From there, the road scraped through 500 miles of steppeland. Once in a while, a pine or birch forest crept into the landscape but we mostly saw grasslands. Endless grasslands.

We got so dirty that, with our fingers, we could write our names in the soot on our skin. What was even worse than this, though, was being attacked by vicious horseflies as big as your

Sunglasses kept the area around Steve's eyes from getting as dirty as the rest of him.

The grasslands and wheat fields stretched for miles along the route to Novosibirsk, a major city in Siberia.

We made a two-day stop in Omsk, a famous manufacturing center that is one of Siberia's biggest cities. We mailed letters and made phone calls. We also sampled some local foods—such as tomato ice cream and *blini,* a doughy pancake served with jam or sour cream.

MORE ABOUT OMSK

Omsk, a famous man-ufacturing and trans-portation center, is also known as the grim prison town that once held one of Russia's greatest writers—Fyodor Dosto-yevsky. The author of the novels *Crime and Punishment* and *The Brothers Karamazov*, Dostoyevsky was im-prisoned in Omsk for criticizing the Russian government.

Sentenced to four years of hard labor in the 1850s, Dostoyevsky later penned *The House of the Dead* to describe his life in Omsk, where he met many types of lawbreakers and villains. He used these contacts to bring a touch of real-ity to his novels, which often include the com-mitting of a crime.

Fyodor Dostoyevsky (1821–1881)

Dan repaired a blown tire not far from Novosibirsk.

We wanted to get to Novosibirsk, a big Siberian city and Volodya's and Alexander's hometown. There we could rest and find parts to fix our rat-tling bicycles. But as we drew to within a day's ride of Novosibirsk, Volodya looked worried. "We still don't know where Alexander is," he reminded me. "What will I tell Alexander's family when I see them?"

At sunset, we rolled into a village to find dinner. In a *produktovi magazin* (grocery store) we bought canned fish, a loaf of bread, and some week-old cookies. When we walked outside again, Alexander stood next to the bikes with out-stretched arms.

"Hi boys!" he shouted. "It's very good to see you."

We embraced and cheered and exchanged

stories. Then Steve pointed at Alexander's brand-new pedal arm, "But how did you find that in the middle of Russia?"

"In Ufa, the boss of a factory helped me," Alexander said. "Two men worked for one whole day to machine me a brand-new pedal arm."

"But what kind of factory makes pedal arms for American mountain bikes?"

"A Russian tank factory."

Steve looked puzzled. "Now that America and Russia are becoming better friends," said Alexander smiling, "the boss said it is wiser for his workers to learn to make something useful."

When Alexander caught up with Dan, Steve, and Volodya outside Novosibirsk, he showed off his new pedal arm.

The members of Sovietrek enjoyed meeting friendly Russians throughout the journey.

AT HOME IN SIBERIA

On July 17—3,245 bicycling miles since entering the Soviet Union—our ragged team rolled into Novosibirsk. The city is located where the **Trans-Siberian railway,** a line that goes from Moscow to Vladivostok, crosses the giant Ob River. Novosibirsk is home to 1.5 million people—including Alexander and Volodya.

Alexander lived on the fourteenth floor of a cement high-rise on the outskirts of the city. His entire apartment—two

40

bedrooms, a family room, a kitchen, and a bathroom—could have fit in the living room of a large American house. He lived there with his wife and his two young children.

Steve and I stayed in Volodya's apartment, with his parents. It, too, was on an upper floor of a high-rise. When we appeared at the door, Volodya's mother, a heavy-set woman with rosy cheeks and her hair up in a bun, hugged us like we were all long-lost sons.

The Trans-Siberian railway, which spans Siberia, passes through Novosibirsk. There once was one line named the Trans-Siberian Railroad, but no single train now holds that title. The Trans-Siberian Express, which goes from Moscow all the way to the Pacific port of Vladivostok, uses some of the old Trans-Siberian Railroad's track during the long trip.

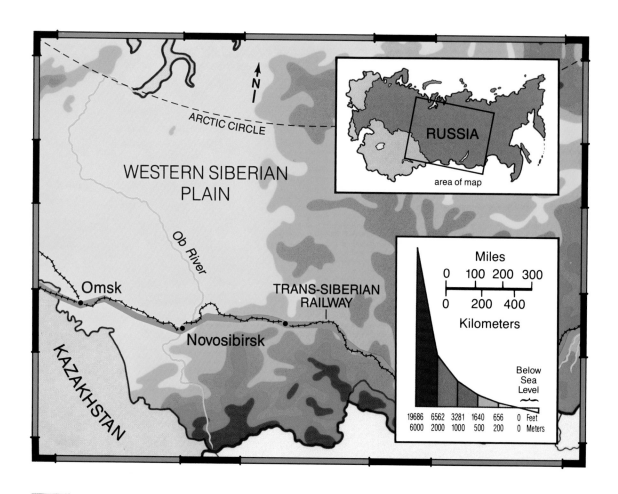

WESTERN SIBERIAN
PLAIN

ARCTIC CIRCLE

RUSSIA

area of map

Ob River

Omsk

TRANS-SIBERIAN
RAILWAY

KAZAKHSTAN

Novosibirsk

Miles
0   100 200 300
0   200   400
Kilometers

Below
Sea
Level

| 19686 | 6562 | 3281 | 1640 | 656 | 0 | Feet |
| 6000 | 2000 | 1000 | 500 | 200 | 0 | Meters |

Sovietrek got a lively welcome in Novosibirsk, the hometown
of Alexander and Volodya. The city's mayor *(standing behind
Steve),* as well as enthusiastic cycling fans, posed in front of the
mayor's office.

Dacha gardens *(above)* are sources of fresh food for many Russian city dwellers, including Volodya's parents, who shared some of their produce *(inset)* with the team.

She hurried us into the apartment and sat us in chairs. As we rested, she washed our clothes and prepared us a feast of meat, mashed potatoes, fresh tomatoes, cucumbers, raspberry jam, and a special treat—sweetened condensed milk.

I told Volodya that I was surprised to see so much fresh food in a big city. "**Dacha** production," Volodya said between mouthfuls. "My mother and father spend all their weekends outside the city, staying in a small cabin, or dacha,

and working in their garden."

The day we left Volodya's house a week later, our clothes were clean, and we were well fed, but we were also anxious to get back on the road. Volodya's mother cried as she waved good-bye.

STEVE'S CLOSE CALL

From Novosibirsk, we bicycled on some of the worst roads yet. We took a turn to the north, biked through a forest, crossed rivers on boats, and spent two days pedaling in mud so thick it caked our brakes and clogged our wheels.

People fed us foods Steve and I had never seen before. A police officer treated us to a jar of warm, fizzy horse's milk. As a present, a construction worker gave us salted fish. An old woman

served us raw eggs that we ate by poking a hole at either end then sucking hard on one of the holes. (It goes down in one gulp.) The oddest dish for Steve and me was *sala*, marshmallow-sized chunks of pig fat eaten cold—hair follicles and all. A true cultural experience!

It was a cool summer evening when we rolled into Krasnoyarsk, our next stop. I was the first to reach the city, which rose quickly out of the Siberian steppe. It reminded me of the Emerald City rising out of the poppy field in *The Wizard of Oz.* But instead of Oz's sparkling, green towers, here the buildings were more of the cement high-rises we'd begun to see in every big Russian city.

On rainy days, mud from unpaved roads spattered the panniers (saddlebags) of trek members and choked their brakes.

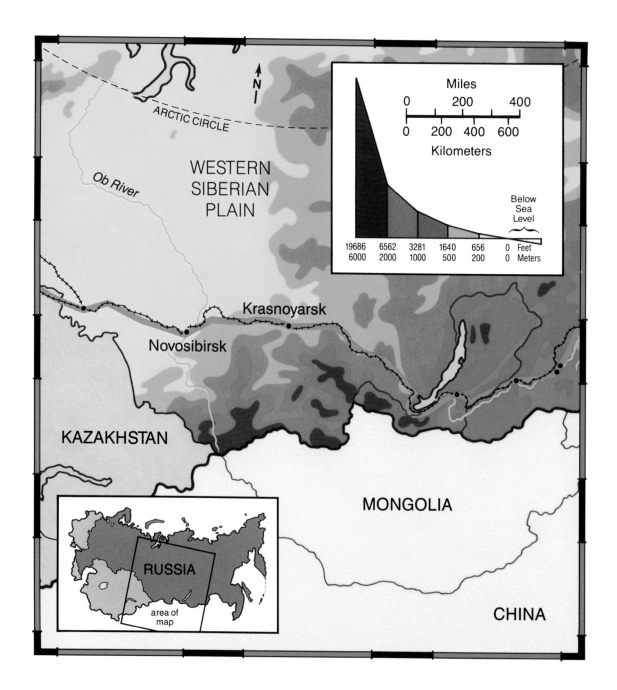

For an American used to the blinking, bright color of U.S. cities, pedaling down one of Krasnoyarsk's streets was like bicycling in a black-and-white movie from the 1950s. Small, dull-colored cars sputtered along the streets, and people on the sidewalks wore clothes that looked like they had seen a lot of wear and tear.

People stood in long lines waiting to get into stores. Posters offered fresh fruit or new shoes or shiny bikes. But in the windows beyond the posters, there was little but empty shelves.

Steve, who was the fastest cyclist of us all,

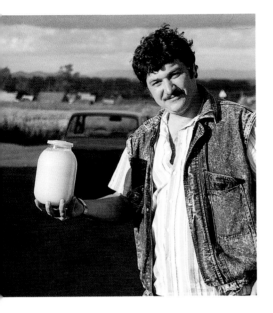

(Far left) An off-duty policeman gave the team a jar of horse's milk. (Left) As the fastest cyclist, Steve often had to wait for the others to catch up.

had been lagging behind all afternoon. I waited for him for two hours before I saw him coming toward me, pushing his bike. He was pale, and sweat beaded his forehead. When he talked, I noticed the back of his tongue had turned black. "I need a bed," he said to me.

We slept in a hotel that night. When Steve awoke the next morning, he was shivering and running a 102° fever. Alexander looked at Steve but was unable to tell what was making him so sick. We decided to call a doctor.

When the doctor arrived, he instantly diagnosed Steve with salmonella—food poisoning. To treat him, the doctor had Steve guzzle three large containers of water, then stick his finger down his throat and throw up! I looked at Alexander, hoping for an explanation of this strange treatment. Alexander shrugged. He looked worried.

The doctor said the treatment might flush out the disease. Instead, the shock to Steve's system was so great that his fever soared to 105°. We called an ambulance.

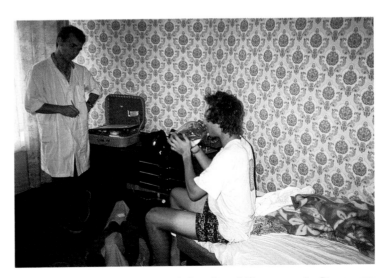

By the time Sovietrek reached the city of Krasnoyarsk, Steve was ill with food poisoning. A doctor told him to drink three large pitchers of water to flush out the disease.

47

The doctor's treatment didn't work, so the team called an ambulance to take Steve to the Krasnoyarsk Regional Hospital *(above)*.

As I waited for the ambulance, I made mental plans to arrange for Steve to fly back to the United States if he got worse. Although Russian medical care was free, I didn't know how it compared to American medical care.

Tall weeds grew on the grounds in front of the Krasnoyarsk Regional Hospital. Inside, it looked like the floor of the emergency room hadn't been swept in a long time. There was an examination table, cloth bandages, alcohol, tongue depressors, and a few metal instruments to treat patients. I missed the computers, electronic equipment, and well-stocked medicine carts you might expect to see in an American emergency room.

Steve's doctor, a woman, was kind and well trained. She knew Steve needed more tests to confirm that salmonella was making him sick and not something more serious. But in Siberia it would take days to get the results.

The medical team wheeled Steve into a stark room. The cement walls, the tile floors, and the lightbulb dangling from the ceiling reminded me of a basement. His nurses, wearing tall, white hats and cloth face masks, gave him injections and tucked him into bed.

The nurses asked me to leave. I went to my brother's bedside. His eyes were dark circles sunken in a putty-white face, his hair a sweaty mass on his head, and a tube led from his arm to a bottle suspended over his head. I felt very helpless.

HIS EYES WERE DARK CIRCLES SUNKEN IN A PUTTY-WHITE FACE, HIS HAIR A SWEATY MASS ON HIS HEAD.

"Come on, Dan," Alexander said softly. "It's better to let him sleep."

The next day, Volodya, Alexander, and I overhauled our bikes, patched up old spare tires, and bought supplies. Late in the afternoon, when the light was best, we struck out on the streets of Krasnoyarsk to take pictures. At suppertime, I called Steve's doctor to get a progress report. "He's sleeping" was all she said.

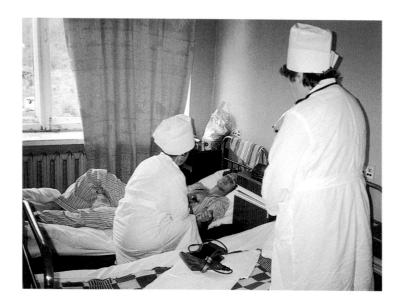

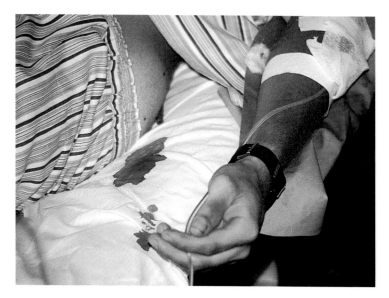

During his stay in the hospital, Steve's nurses checked his heart *(top)* and hooked him up to a feeding tube *(above)*.

49

I returned two days later to find that Steve was still running a fever but was out of danger. His nurses had grown to like him and had given him special favors, including soft toilet paper and a spoon for eating his porridge. (In Russia, old newspapers often double as toilet paper, and in many hospitals patients must bring their own silverware.)

After seven days, Steve was much better. His fever had left him, and he was anxious to get back on his bike. But the doctors wouldn't release him. I asked the

While Steve recovered, Alexander, Volodya, and Dan explored Krasnoyarsk. They toured a Russian Orthodox church *(above)* **and visited a flowerseller's market stall** *(right).*

Steve bounced back, and soon Sovietrek was on the road again.

reason of Alexander, who as a biologist had frequently worked with doctors.

"Russian doctors," Alexander explained, "are often paid less than factory workers. Because Steve is the first American in this hospital, he is a very important person."

"So?"

"If Steve's doctor lets him out and tomorrow he comes back sick, the doctor will get in big trouble from the hospital director. So, it's easier for the doctor just to keep Steve here."

We waited three more days, then Volodya, Alexander, and I went to visit Steve. He had been well for a long time, so we asked the doctor to let us take Steve on a walk in the hospital courtyard. On the way out of the room, we grabbed Steve's bag. That was the last we saw of the Krasnoyarsk Regional Hospital.

AN AWESOME LAKE

From Krasnoyarsk, we entered Buryatia. The Buryat, one of Russia's many Asian ethnic groups, had lived in this area for hundreds of years before the Soviet government made it an official ethnic region.

Every 20 miles or so, we'd find a Buryat village, where we'd fill our water bottles at a well. If we arrived at midday, we'd eat lunch in a *stolovaya* (cafeteria). Everywhere we stopped, we drew crowds of curious kids.

ДОБРО ПОЖАЛОВАТЬ!

First, one or two boys would approach and cautiously ask us where we were from. Soon, we'd hear *"Americanski, Americanski!"* ring through the streets and before we knew it we were mobbed by boys and girls.

The girls wore colorful dresses with big white bows in their hair. The boys wore plain trousers and button-down shirts. They flooded us with questions. "How far have you ridden your bike?" "What do American children think of Russian children?" It was hard to make good answers. But between the four of us, we tried.

Schoolchildren swarmed around Alexander and Steve during a stop at an elementary school.

The flat farmland that we had long passed through now gave way to evergreen forests. The state-run **collective farms** we saw increasingly lacked equipment. Wells replaced running water, horse-drawn carts substituted for automobiles, and almost every rural dwelling was a log house, called an *isba.*

After spending the morning winding and rolling over a road through thick pine forests, we climbed one last hill and coasted with ease around a bend. Our ONC maps told us we were about to take in something very unique. Then we glimpsed the sparkling blue waters of Lake Baikal stretching all the way to the horizon. I stopped to take pictures but realized no single photograph could capture this incredible scene.

Pour yourself five glasses of water. If the water in those glasses represented all the freshwater on earth, one whole glass would belong to Lake Baikal.

Lake Baikal is more than a mile deep. If you emptied the lake, it would take all the rivers of the world flowing for one year to fill it back up. What makes it so deep? Lake Baikal sits on a huge rift, or crack in the earth. The crack is getting

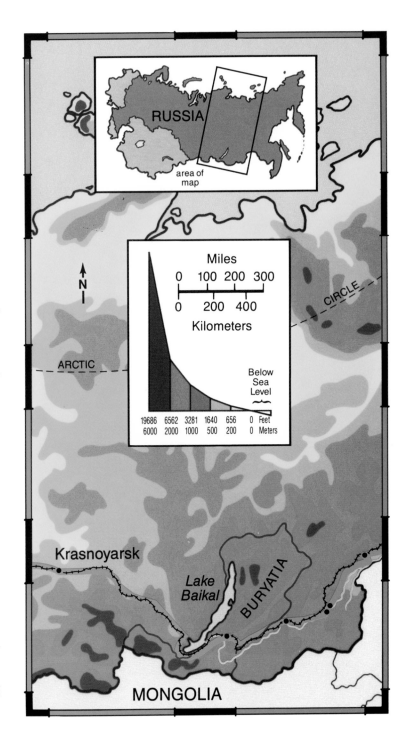

Volodya and Steve rounded a bend to reach Lake Baikal.

The deepest lake on earth, Baikal holds about 20 percent of the world's unfrozen freshwater. More than 300 rivers flow into the lake, but only one—the Angara River—flows out.

about an inch wider every year. As a result, the bottom gets deeper and sediment collects on the lake floor.

We sped down the hillside. As we neared the water, it changed in color from deep blue to crystal, clear green. On all sides, the tree-lined shore rose quickly to mile-high mountains, some of which we thought were extinct volcanoes.

Volodya, Steve, Alexander, and I were pedaling along the shore, enjoying the scenery when we came upon the Baikalsk Cellulose-Paper Mill. Long plumes of black smoke poured from the factory's towering chimneys. This scene reminded me that Lake Baikal's unique environment may not last forever.

I had read that the factory's chemical wastes are dumped into the water. Untreated sewage and other factory wastes come into the lake from Baikal's hundreds of inflowing rivers. The chemicals have killed off all plant life on 23 square miles of the lake's floor. Some say the damage can't be fixed. As we looked at the beauty of the scenery, we could only hope that that forecast was false.

Lake Baikal is home to several unique animals, including the Baikal seal (right inset). **Smoke billows from the Baikalsk Cellulose-Paper Mill** (left inset). **Chemical wastes from the factory stream into the lake and endanger its wildlife.**

BURYAT BRILLIANCE

As Lake Baikal faded from view, we pedaled eastward toward Ulan-Ude, the Buryat capital city. Like other ethnic groups in Siberia, the Buryat are officially Russian, but they maintain their traditional customs, languages, and religions. Ulan-Ude, for example, holds a Buddhist monastery, where monks are trained to guide the Buryat in Buddhist religious beliefs.

Five miles outside of Ulan-Ude, I felt a curious bumping in my rear tire. Then POP! Sssssss. I looked down to see that not only had I blown a tire, but the aluminum rim of my rear wheel was completely cracked. A flat tire wasn't a problem because I carried patches. But I couldn't fix an aluminum rim. And the closest place to buy a new one was in Tokyo, 3,200 miles away!

The Asian city of Ulan-Ude, the capital of Buryatia, has several religious buildings where *lamas* **(monks) teach Buddhist beliefs to the Buryat people.**

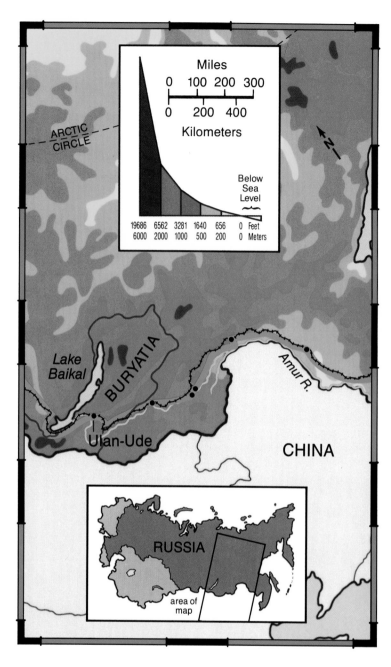

We stopped to talk about a solution. Ulan-Ude had both a train station and an airport. Volodya suggested I take a train to Moscow and look for a new wheel there. Alexander thought I wouldn't find a wheel in Moscow, and it would be better to try to fly to Tokyo. Either solution would take weeks.

Just then, we noticed a bicyclist coming toward us riding a really good racing bike. We waved for him to stop. Speaking Russian with a Buryat accent, he told us his name was Sasha. Seeing a glimmer of hope for my cracked wheel, I asked him in an excited voice, "Where did you find that bike?"

"I built it myself," he replied, "from tubes I got at a nearby fighter jet factory."

"Do you think you can fix my wheel?"

He bent down. The rim was hopelessly split in two. "Of course," he said. "Follow me."

Young Buryat enjoy a refreshing stroll on a sunny day in Ulan-Ude.

Sasha led us to his house. In a back alley, he opened a garage door to reveal a makeshift bike factory. There was a drill, a sander, a welder, a few hand tools, and a pickup truck full of wrecked bicycle parts. He dug through the pile and pulled out a broken bicycle wheel that I knew was 30 inches around. I shook my head at him.

Just outside Ulan-Ude, Dan ran into equipment trouble—a flat tire and a cracked wheel rim *(right)*. After taking off the tire, Steve *(above)* looked at the extent of the damage, which Sasha *(in the background)*, a self-taught bike mechanic, had luckily offered to fix.

"No way!" I said. "You'll never get that 30-inch wheel on my mountain bike frame. My frame's only big enough to fit a 26-inch wheel."

"Watch me," he said.

I was about to be amazed by Buryat inge-nuity. Sasha snipped all of the spokes out of the Russian wheel. He then cut out a four-inch section from the rim and squeezed it back into a circle. By melting the metal from a clothes hanger, he welded the

Sasha first clipped out the spokes *(left)* from an old wheel that was larger than Dan's destroyed wheel. With Volodya's aid, Sasha then cut out a section of metal *(below)* from the bigger wheel, which Steve helped him match *(bottom)* to the size of Dan's bike.

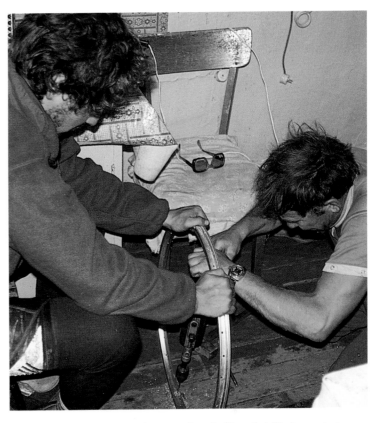

Sasha next welded the rim together *(left)* and drilled new holes for the spokes *(above)*. He stood at the doorway of his workshop *(below left)*, as Dan tried out his new wheel *(below right)*.

rim back together. He then drilled 36 new holes and replaced the spokes. When Sasha was done, I had a wheel much stronger than the one I had had before.

I thanked him as much as I could. He had saved Sovietrek for me. As I pedaled away, I thought that if Sasha represented the ingenuity of the Buryat people, maybe Lake Baikal had a chance of surviving.

ALEXANDER'S UNLUCKY ADVENTURE

We found a surprisingly good road when we pedaled out of Ulan-Ude. It followed the Khilok River, ran through the Yablonovy Mountains, and reached Chita, another large Siberian city. Then we entered Nerchinsk, a mining town that was one of the first Russian outposts in eastern Asia.

As I pedaled along the road with ease, I thought about how much sense it makes to travel by bicycle. On a bicycle, you go slowly enough to get a feel for what it's like to live in the different regions you pass through. You not only see your surroundings, but you hear, feel, and smell them, too.

A member of the team enjoyed the scenery while biking through rural Siberia.

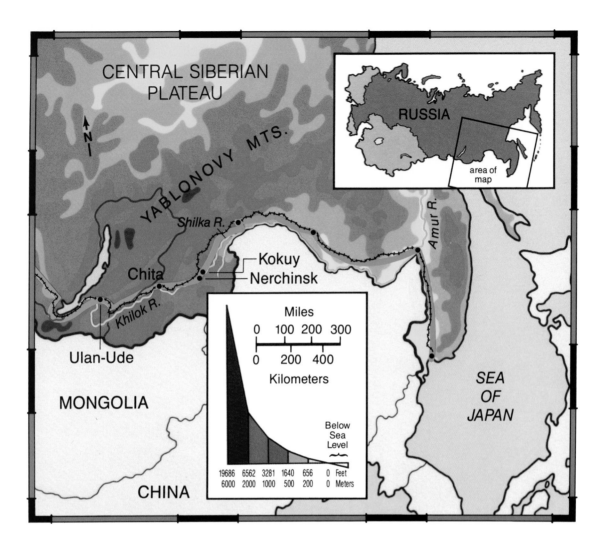

When you stop during your travels, people are curious, and they ask questions. Sometimes they invite you into their homes. Every day, as the road unfolds, you're greeted by a mixture of adventures, peoples, and landscapes.

But what happens when the road stops? Unfortunately, we were about to find out. Fifty miles east of Nerchinsk, the pavement ended and a dirt road began. When it rained, we biked through mud.

For Alexander, this stretch of the trek was particularly hard. Cycling down a steep, slippery hill, his front wheel slid out from under him. He did a complete somersault, with his feet still in the pedals, and landed hard on his side. I heard the thud and then his agonized groan.

I squeezed my brakes hard and doubled back. Alexander was lying on the ground, motionless. My first thought was "Oh my God, he's dead." But when I got closer, I could see he was just staring up at the sky.

"Are you all right?" I asked urgently.

"I think I'm fine," he replied softly. "Maybe some problem with my arm." I helped Alexander fix his front wheel, and within an hour he was back on his bike.

But I noticed over the next two days that he biked using only one arm. The other arm dangled limply at his side. Every time I asked him about it, he responded, "No problem, it's just a little bit sore."

But it was more than just sore. Two days after the fall, he came to breakfast with his arm cradled in a sling fashioned from a T-shirt. "I think, finally, my arm is broken," he said.

Again, the team discussed options. The nearest hospital was 70 miles away, and there was no public transportation. It was late August. Siberia's autumn freeze would be upon us soon, and the most challenging part of the trek—the bog—still lay ahead.

We also knew that the road would come to an end in a few hundred miles, in a town called Kokuy on the banks of the Shilka River. There, we would have to spend a few days preparing for the roadless part of Siberia. We'd have to find food and supplies, secure police permission, and, if the terrain was impassable, build a raft for floating down the river.

Steve offered to help Alexander get to the hospital, but Alexander said no. "I must hitchhike," he said. "It's much easier for one person to find a ride than for two. Thanks, Steve, for your offer, but you must go to Kokuy and help prepare for the bog. Later, I will catch up with you." We didn't much like the choices, but we knew he was right. Steve, Volodya, and I rode on.

Alexander was an experienced, steady cyclist. During this part of the trek, however, when the rain-drenched dirt roads were slippery with mud, Alexander flipped over and broke his arm. He hitchhiked to the nearest town to have it set in a cast.

67

ROLLING ON THE RIVERS

As we pedaled toward Kokuy, forests of birch and pine lined the road, with here and there a small settlement. When we did find a village, food was scarce, except for the fruits and vegetables offered from a family garden. Then, in Kokuy, the road stopped altogether. Mud was everywhere. I remembered Vladimir, who'd invited us in out of the rain at Sernovodsk and who'd thought we'd never make it across Siberia's

bogs and swamps. After this much brute effort, however, I wasn't about to give up.

In Kokuy, soldiers told us we couldn't continue overland. Our only choice was to build rafts and float down the Shilka River for about 250 miles, to where we'd be able to pick up the road again near the town of Yerofey-Pavlovich.

Apartment buildings in Kokuy line one side of the Shilka River. Paddling down the waterway in small boats was the only way the team could reach the town of Yerofey-Pavlovich, 250 miles away.

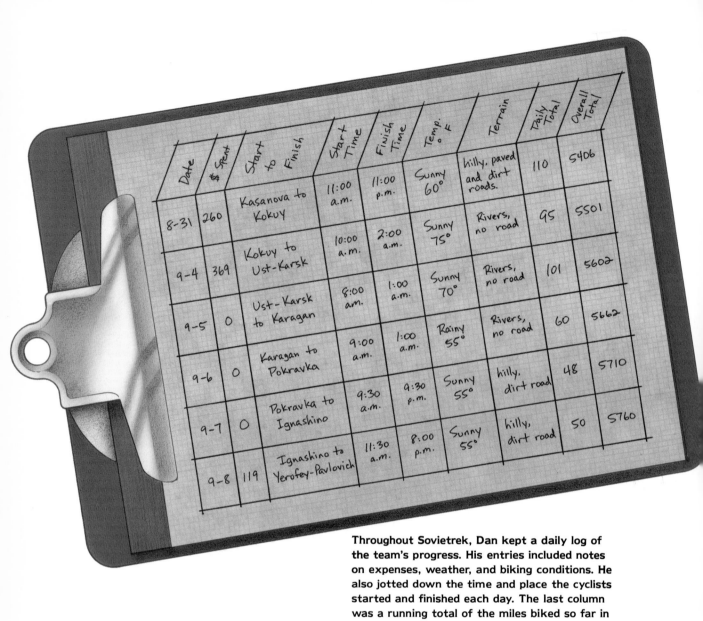

Date	$ Spent	Start to Finish	Start Time	Finish Time	Temp. °F	Terrain	Daily Total	Overall Total
8-31	260	Kasanova to Kokuy	11:00 a.m.	11:00 p.m.	Sunny 60°	hilly, paved and dirt roads.	110	5406
9-4	369	Kokuy to Ust-Karsk	10:00 a.m.	2:00 a.m.	Sunny 75°	Rivers, no road	95	5501
9-5	0	Ust-Karsk to Karagan	8:00 am.	1:00 a.m.	Sunny 70°	Rivers, no road	101	5602
9-6	0	Karagan to Pokravka	9:00 a.m.	1:00 a.m.	Rainy 55°	Rivers, no road	60	5662
9-7	0	Pokravka to Ignashino	9:30 a.m.	9:30 p.m.	Sunny 55°	hilly, dirt road	48	5710
9-8	119	Ignashino to Yerofey-Pavlovich	11:30 a.m.	8:00 p.m.	Sunny 55°	hilly, dirt road	50	5760

Throughout Sovietrek, Dan kept a daily log of the team's progress. His entries included notes on expenses, weather, and biking conditions. He also jotted down the time and place the cyclists started and finished each day. The last column was a running total of the miles biked so far in the Soviet Union.

We first tried to build rafts out of plywood and inner tubes. They proved to be too shaky, so we turned to abandoned military lifeboats. The boats were brittle and in serious need of repair.

The soldier who offered them to us had said, "They're yours if you want them, but I wouldn't float down the Shilka River in them. The Shilka can get pretty rough."

We spent three days repairing the boats' holes. We made oars for each boat out of pipes and sheet metal and built wooden platforms so we'd have a raised, dry place to sleep. We calculated that the trip down the Shilka would take four days.

We scoured the town for supplies. Except for bread and porridge, we found nothing in the town's stores. Kokuy's mayor—a young man who longed for adventure—helped us. He brought us to a military warehouse and got us cans of sardines, condensed milk, and pork fat.

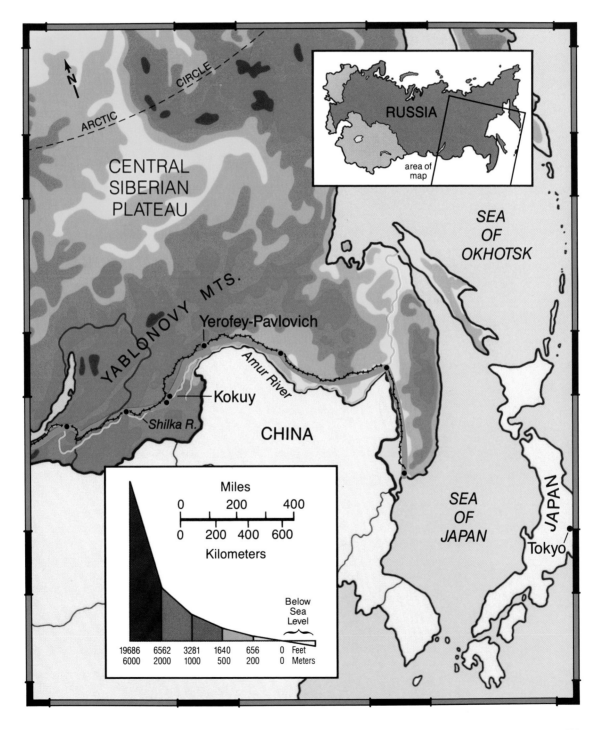

On our fourth day in Kokuy, we got a pleasant surprise when Alexander rolled into town with a cast on his arm. He did his best to help us load the boats with the food, bikes, and equipment.

We found the best way to distribute the total weight of our supplies. Steve, Alexander, I, and our bikes piled into one boat, while Volodya traveled with his bike and most of the other equipment in a second boat.

The coffee-with-cream-colored water swirled around us, and the swift current pushed us quickly downstream. Our rafts floated beside steep cliffs and green forests. Occasionally, we'd see isbas with thin wisps of smoke curling out of their chimneys. Because we were behind schedule, we stayed in our boats from morning to evening, stopping only at suppertime to cook a meal over a small campfire. At night, Steve, Alexander, and I took turns steering the raft while the others slept.

My watch was between 2:00 A.M. and 4:00 A.M. I sat at the back of the boat, steering with the oars and bundled

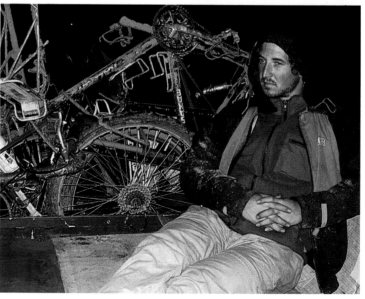

(Left) **Alexander rejoined the team in Kokuy with his arm in a cast. Eventually, he took it off so he could move his arm more easily.**
(Above) **Steve relaxed during a nighttime trip down the Shilka.**

up against the night air. There was a full moon, and its reflection cast a silvery ribbon on the waters. Along the river-bank, I could see the outline of treetops against the light sky. At times I could hear the faraway trumpeting of a reindeer.

It was a magical journey in the Siberian wilderness. Nothing could go wrong. We were safe, or so I thought.

(Above) **From the river, the team saw small, wooden houses along the shore.** *(Inset)* **Volodya and a Russian cyclist who joined Sovietrek for a time ate a snack in one of the lifeboats.**

MUD, MUD, AND MORE MUD

After a long wait at the border, the soldiers did let us through. We traveled north to the town of Yerofey-Pavlovich. It was mainly a collection of isbas and cement buildings near the Trans-Siberian railway.

The railroad runs more than 5,000 miles from Moscow across the Ural Mountains to the Pacific Ocean. It takes seven days and nights to travel that distance. As a result, the line's conductors, engineers, and other train workers are away from home for two weeks at a time. For them, Yerofey-Pavlovich is a place where they can get a hot meal and a comfortable bed.

Volodya followed Alexander down a muddy track into the wilds of Siberia.

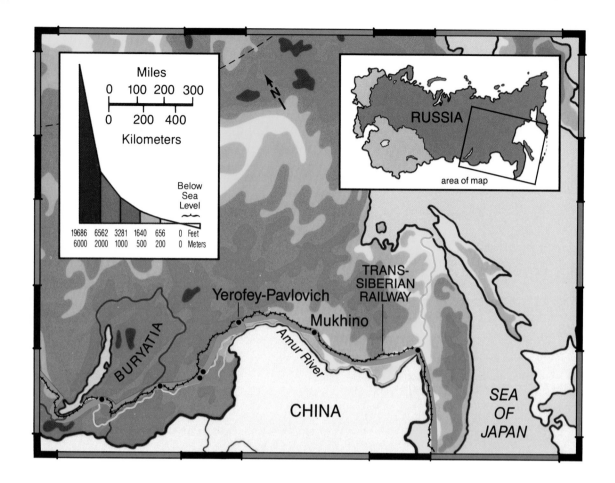

We followed a conductor into the stolovaya, where waiters served us a meal of meatloaf, cold noodles, cabbage, sour cream, and warm juice made from birch sap. After lunch, we bought supplies at the grocery store, mostly buckwheat porridge and pig fat.

When we pedaled out of town, we knew we were headed into the wilds of Siberia. But we had no idea how wild they would be.

It all started with mud—mushy, brown muck that looked and felt like thick chocolate pudding. At first, we could ride through it. The mud made a pleasant crackle under our tires, like the sound of masking tape being pulled off a wall.

But every couple of minutes my front tire would throw up a fat glob of mud that would hit my face with a cold THWACK! I'd pedal harder. Sometimes the glob flew

right into my mouth— and believe me the mud didn't *taste* like chocolate pudding.

Three days after leaving Yerofey-Pavlovich, the mud was so deep that we could no longer ride through it. So we pushed our bikes. This effort was like trying to push a grocery cart full of watermelons through deep sand. Our bicycle wheels sunk to the hubs, and our feet disappeared into the cold wet earth with every step. Sometimes our shoes got stuck, and we'd have to reach down into the last footprint to retrieve them.

For several days we found our only drinking water in dirty puddles. When we got thirsty, we dipped our water bottles down and let them fill with a gurgle. To purify the muddy water and to keep from getting sick, we put three drops of iodine into each bottleful. This is the same stuff my mom used to put on my cuts. Food was scarce. Breakfast, lunch, and dinner consisted of the same meal—pig fat porridge and muddy water. Yum.

Mud clogged the roadless section of the trek. *(Below left)* Steve struggled to pedal through the muck that seemed to reach to the horizon. *(Below)* Sometimes the bikes became completely mired in wet soil.

When team members weren't pedaling through mud, they were crossing icy rivers.

Sometimes we came to short rivers or shallow streams. There was usually no bridge, and the water ran crystal clear and icy cold. To cross the rivers, we got a running start then we'd speed into the water, spraying wide jets from our wheels.

Once we came to a river that was almost as wide as a city block. We walked along the shore for several miles until we came to the Trans-Siberian railway, where we found a bridge. We scrambled up a hill and were about to cross the bridge when a soldier

stepped out of a small guardhouse. He aimed his machine gun at us.

"Halt!" he shouted. "What are you doing here?"

We froze. After a long terrifying moment, Alexander stuttered, "Ah...er... we are an American-Soviet team biking across Russia."

The soldier didn't lower his gun. Maybe he didn't believe us. After we showed him our papers, he let us cross the bridge.

I couldn't really blame him for stopping us. In this region, soldiers guard railroad bridges

If streams were shallow enough, the team could cycle across them.

in the unlikely event of a Chinese attack. Since there's no road, the Trans-Siberian railway transports almost everything. So a blown-up bridge could seriously slow traffic between eastern and western Russia.

Besides small units of soldiers, we didn't see many people in this part of Russia. Most villages consisted of a few small isbas next to the railroad tracks. There were no schools, public buildings, or even stores.

Sometimes it was easier to carry the bikes from one riverbank to the other.

Soldiers were more common than houses or towns in this part of Siberia, which borders China.

vodka, and other things that they couldn't produce at home, they'd buy in the "train store," a sort of shopping mall on wheels that stopped only twice a month.

Every morning we'd wake early. All day long, we'd heave our bikes and sink to our knees in mud. At any moment, we could look behind us and still see where we'd been an hour earlier. At the end of a 14-hour day, we'd study our map only to realize that we'd come just 10 or 11 miles. Less than one mile per hour! After a couple of days of being constantly wet, our legs became white and wrinkled, like your fingertips after a hot bath.

Eventually, the mud gave way to swamp. I had heard that in the winter when everything was frozen, the route we followed was a road. With some imagination, you could see the faint outline of a road in the

While passing through a boggy field, Steve (below) **covered his legs to protect them from stickers. Alexander** (below right) **pushed his bike through the same field.**

The people made their living by keeping the train tracks in good repair. For food, they'd plant plots the size of swimming pools with tomatoes, onions, cucumbers, sunflowers, raspberries, strawberries, and potatoes. Shoes, clothes, tools, tea, sugar,

The field gave way to swampland that was nearly impossible to pedal through, so Steve *(above)* pulled his bike along behind him. Not far from the town of Mukhino, Alexander *(below)* walked his bike beside the tracks of the Trans-Siberian railway.

reeds and pools of water in front of us. But it was easier to see swamp. Swamp as far as you could see. I again thought of Vladimir.

Over and over, we'd ask ourselves, "Are we really going to make it?" Then we'd look at one another and realize we couldn't give up. People throughout the United States and Russia had helped us get this far. Our families had backed us in our dream to make this trek. And we'd come to depend on one another. Heads down, we returned to our task.

The swamp finally ended in a small town called Mukhino. More than a thousand miles of bad road stood between us and Vladivostok, the Russian seaport on the Pacific coast that marked the end of our journey. After the bog, though, anything seemed easy.

CYCLING BY THE CLOCK

Pedaling out of the bog was an enormous relief. It felt like an elephant had just jumped off my shoulders. But over the next 1,169 miles, as the dirt road gave way to gravel and finally to pavement, hardship and adventure were replaced by boredom and routine.

The scenery returned to the wheat fields that had dominated the landscape earlier in the trek. All the log homes and villages began to look the same. Getting on

our bikes each morning started to feel like punching the time clock at a factory job. We'd pedal for 60 miles in the morning, stop at a stolovaya for lunch at noon, and take an hour's nap. Then we'd bike about 40 miles until sunset, when we'd knock at a door and, to our constant surprise, be invited into a Russian home.

Despite the drudgery of this part of the trek, Steve and I never tired of meeting Russian people. Their lives were so different from our own. Sometimes, to us, the living conditions seemed unbearably hard.

Throughout the journey, trek members enjoyed the hospitality of Russian families.

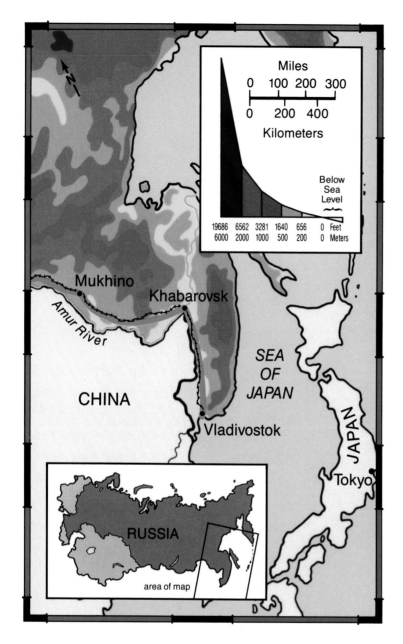

People stood in long lines for food. Sugar or a can of condensed milk was a once-a-month treat.

But Steve and I also saw many positive things. What seemed most important to Russians was spending time with their families. After dinner, the family sat around the kitchen table and discussed the events of

WHAT SEEMED MOST IMPORTANT TO RUSSIANS WAS SPENDING TIME WITH THEIR FAMILIES.

the day. They played checkers and chess. They sang songs for entertainment and read the works of their country's great writers.

Russians always took great pride in their gardens—and for good reasons. Private gardens were often the only sources of fresh food, which we'd enjoyed throughout the trek.

If the people lived in the country, empty stores meant they had to depend on their own gardening skills for most of their food. Their wood or cement houses rarely had indoor plumbing, a fact that created a chilly walk to the outhouse during the long Siberian winters.

Conditions also seemed tough if the people lived in the city, where an average family of four stayed in a small, two-bedroom apartment.

(Left) Farmers pause while harvesting their crop of potatoes in eastern Siberia. (Below) Standing in his garden, a worker on a state-owned farm drinks water from the well behind his house.

harvest early." The worries of potato farmers seemed the same whether they worked in Siberia or in Idaho.

If people lived in the country, their gardens were in the backyard. City folk would spend their summer weekends at their dacha gardens.

I found that if I was at a loss for conversation, the subject of potatoes would often spark a lively discussion. "Potato crop good this year?" I might begin. "Not bad, but worms are starting to creep in," answered one Siberian woman I chatted with. "I might have to

When our sorry bicycles rolled into the city of Khabarovsk, they were rattling and creaking like whining goats. The wheels were bent, our tires were worn out, and Alexander's front rack was cracked and ready to snap off. Although Khabarovsk was a regional capital of more than 600,000 people, there were no bike parts to be found.

We were again very lucky because we met several members of a bicycling club—guys ranging in age from 12 to 82—who seemed to live to pedal. With typical Russian hospitality, they adopted us. Although their bike shop had few tools, they worked with us for three days and nights to make our bikes ready for the last leg of Sovietrek.

Outside the city of Khabarovsk, Russian laborers examined Dan's muddy, rattling mountain bike.

They welded Alexander's rack and made new spokes for us out of lengths of wire. They fixed our flattened tires by cutting out good sections of their old tires and gluing them into the inside of ours. When we left, all they would take for their work was a Sovietrek T-shirt. "This is a souvenir we will always remember," said the club president. It seemed to us that we got the better end of the deal.

Back on the road, Steve and I really began to miss home. Since leaving Minnesota, we'd pedaled more than 10,000 miles and had lived on the go for almost 200 days. We wanted to see our families, talk to our friends, and sleep in our own beds. We longed for news and to hear the latest rock and roll.

"What do you miss most?" I asked Steve on one chilly evening around sunset as we were pedaling side by side. "Right now," he replied slightly out of breath, "I'd love a slice of pepperoni pizza." I knew just how he felt.

KEEPING TRACK

✓ Greatest number of miles biked in a day: 129 on August 24

✓ Fewest number of miles biked in a day: 12 on September 18

✓ Total number of times the team pushed its bike pedals: 5.6 million

✓ Total number of calories burned by each biker: 450,000

✓ Total number of flat tires: 350

✓ Average number of Russian words Dan learned each day: 20

✓ Number of times the team was invited to stay in a Russian home: 100

While he cycled, Dan studied a list of Russian words that was mounted on his handlebars.

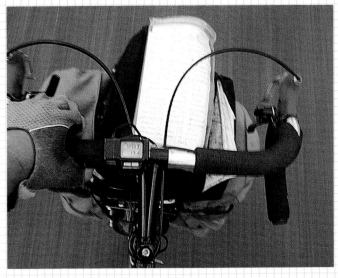

VLADIVOSTOK OR BUST

During the final week of the trek, we bicycled on a very good road. We traveled southward on a finger of land surrounded by China on one side and the Pacific Ocean on the other. This was no longer Siberia. Now we were in Russia's Pacific coastal region.

It was October. All the crops had been harvested, and haystacks dotted the fields. When the road took us through forests, they reminded Steve and me of Minnesota.

Birch and oak trees were wearing their autumn colors, and our bikes rolled over a carpet of fallen leaves. The difference between the forests of Minnesota and these forests was that here Siberian tigers still prowled. One farmer we met complained that tigers had killed two of his cows.

Fall was changing the leaves of trees near Vladivostok, the port that marked the easternmost point of Sovietrek.

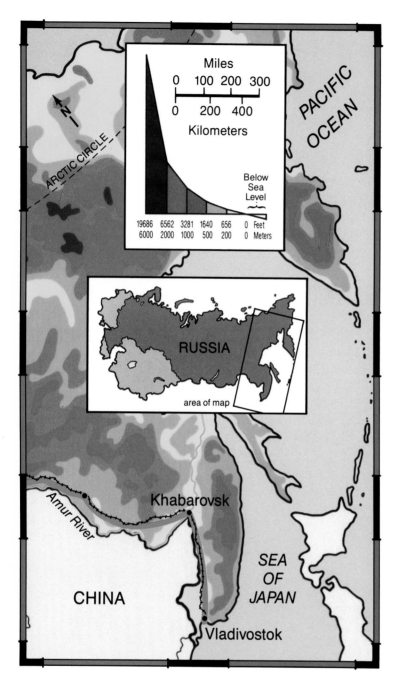

Map labels:
Miles
0 100 200 300
0 200 400
Kilometers

Below Sea Level

19686 6562 3281 1640 656 0 Feet
6000   2000 1000 500   200 0 Meters

N

ARCTIC CIRCLE

PACIFIC OCEAN

RUSSIA

area of map

Amur River

Khabarovsk

CHINA

SEA OF JAPAN

Vladivostok

photographs. In the 124 days we'd been in the Soviet Union, we'd biked 7,353 miles, a distance equal to crossing the continental United States two and a half times.

Although we were dirty, with creaking bicycles and ripped panniers, we were happy. But in our minds our journey wouldn't be complete until we dipped our front wheels in the Pacific Ocean. This body of water was on the other side of Vladivostok. My partners and I glided down one final hill to the blue Pacific Ocean. We pushed our bikes onto the beach and then into the water.

As Alexander, Steve, Volodya, and I watched the sun go down over the Pacific Ocean, the sky was shimmering with red and orange colors. We all knew that our journey wasn't over. We still had to make it home. But as we watched the setting sun, we were all thinking the same thing— what an incredible adventure!

Tigers were far from my mind one afternoon when I saw Steve waving his arms at me from a spot up ahead. "We made it!" he yelled. I squeezed my brakes.

Volodya, Alexander, and Steve had leaned their bikes against a huge sign in Russian that read "Vladivostok." We jumped and cheered, hugged one another, and took

Alexander, Steve, and Dan posed at the Vladivostok city limit on October 6, 1990.

In Vladivostok the four members of Sovietrek pushed their bikes into the Sea of Japan, an arm of the Pacific Ocean.

EPILOGUE

Sovietrek had a couple more stops after the team reached Vladivostok. Alexander, Steve, Volodya, and I flew some 18,000 miles through Moscow, Germany, and New York before getting back on our bikes in Los Angeles, California. From there, we pedaled 2,200 miles in 22 days and finished our journey where we'd started it—in Minnesota. We biked 12,888 miles in 239 days. We'd set a world record for the Soviet leg of the trek.

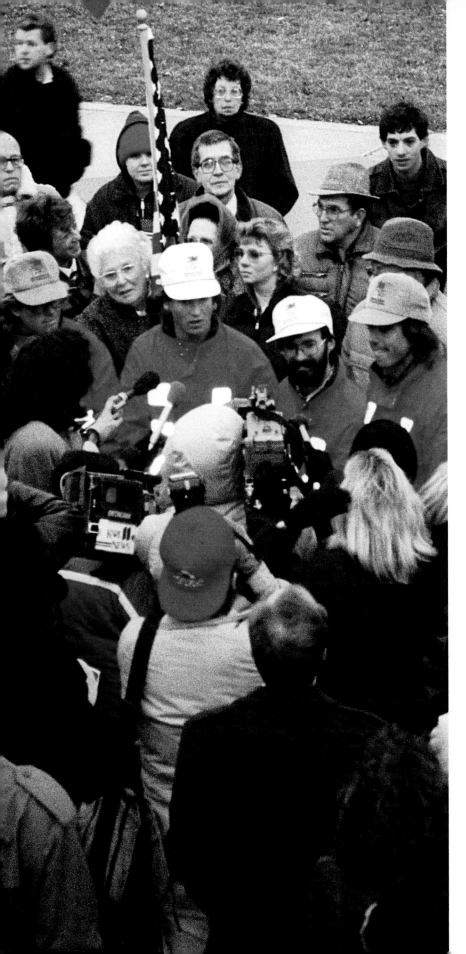

Although I was finally home, memories of Sovietrek raced through my head. The big Russian cities were full of cement high-rises, but at street level, you couldn't help but enjoy the outdoor markets, the street vendors, and the many faces of the Russian people. In autumn the countryside was ablaze with golden fields, green pine forests, multicolored wildflowers, and the fiery hues of autumn leaves.

A throng of well-wishers, photographers, and journalists crowded around the team upon its return to Minnesota in November 1990.

95

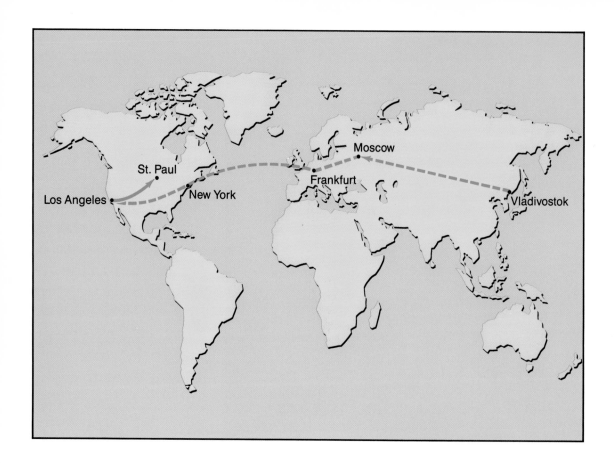

And the Russian people were unbelievably hospitable. Of the more than 120 nights we spent in the Soviet Union, we were invited into people's homes at least 100 times. Friendly, generous Russians gave us food, warmth, and shelter. They shared with us a slice of life that had been a mystery to most Americans for more than 70 years.

Were Russians happy? I had asked this question of almost everyone I

In rural areas, some of the most attractive Russian houses are *isbas*, small log homes with ornately decorated windows.

met during Sovietrek. Most people answered yes. Sure, they complained of long lines and food shortages. But it sounded to me like the harsh living conditions brought people together and made them more willing to help one another.

(Left) **Men and women help drive home the cows in a Siberian village.** *(Below left)* **Dan followed an old Russian custom by tying a piece of cloth to a tree for luck.** *(Below right)* **Volodya and Alexander got directions from helpful Russians.**

(Left) **Villagers line up for the daily delivery of bread.** *(Below)* **A guitarist entertained team members in Siberia.**

One of the main things that seemed to make Russians happy was having free time. Although Russians earn less money than Americans do, Russians work fewer hours. They have more chances to be with their families and friends. They spend more time in their gardens and fewer hours in front of a television. They read and sing for entertainment.

The boss of a collective farm said to me, "We respect America and all the wonderful things you have. But we have our own culture, and we wouldn't trade that for all the dollars in the world." I admired him for speaking his mind. Maybe that's where everything begins between people from different worlds—with mutual respect for one another's way of life.

(Above) **At an outdoor event, a babushka shows off her granddaughter.** *(Right)* **A woman collects water at a communal well.** *(Far right)* **In his spare time, a worker on the Trans-Siberian railway digs potatoes from his garden.**

PRONUNCIATION GUIDE

babushka	BAH-boosh-kuh
banya	BAH-nyah
blini	blee-NEE
borscht	BOORSCH
Cyrillic	suh-RIHL-ik
dacha	DATCH-uh
gribi	gree-BEE
isba	ihz-BAH
izvinite	eez-vih-NEE-tyeh
Khabarovsk	kuh-BAHR-uhfsk
Krasnoyarsk	krahs-nuh-YAHRSK
Kuibyshev	KOO-ee-buh-shehf
nevozmozhni	nyeh-vohz-MOHZ-noh
Novosibirsk	no-vo-suh-BIRSK
otkuda	aht-KOO-duh
produktovi magazin	proh-DOOK-toh-vee mah-guh-ZEEN
sala	SAH-loh
Siber	sih-BIHR
stolovaya	stah-LO-vuh-yuh
studen	STOO-den
taiga	TY-guh
Ufa	oo-FAH
Ulan-Ude	oo-lahn—oo-DAY
Vladivostok	vlah-dee-vuh-STAHK
Volodya	vuh-LO-dyuh
Yablonovy	yahb-luh-nuh-VEE
Yerofey-Pavlovich	yeh-roh-FAY—PAH-vloh-vitch
zdrazstzuite	ZDRAST-vooee-tyeh

A vendor offers a jar of blueberries to passersby.

GLOSSARY

Asian Russia: the section of Russia east of the Ural Mountains that is part of the Asian continent.

banya: a Russian sauna that is also a place to bathe.

collective farm: a large farming estate worked by a group. The workers usually receive a portion of the farm's harvest as wages. On a Soviet collective farm, the central government in Moscow owned the land, buildings, and machinery.

dacha: a Russian country cottage that is often located just outside the city limits. Most dachas have large gardens in the backyard, where families grow vegetables and fruits.

European Russia: the section of Russia west of the Ural Mountains that is part of the European continent.

isba: a single-story log house common in Siberia that is often decorated with ornate wooden carving.

pannier: a bag, usually one of a pair, carried on either side of a bicycle.

rapids: the part of a river where the current flows with more than normal swiftness.

Volodya struggled to guide his bike down a rocky hill.

METRIC CONVERSION CHART		
WHEN YOU KNOW:	**MULTIPLY BY:**	**TO FIND:**
teaspoon	15.0	milliliters
Tablespoon	5.0	milliliters
quarts	.95	liters
pounds	.454	kilograms
inches	2.54	centimeters
miles	1.609	kilometers
square miles	2.59	square kilometers
degrees Fahrenheit	5/9 (after subtracting 32)	degrees Celsius

Steve and Alexander cycled along an unpaved road near the city of Chita.

Siberia: a region of Russia that stretches from the Ural Mountains eastward to the Pacific Ocean. Siberia's northern boundary is the Arctic Ocean. To the south lie Kazakhstan, China, and Mongolia.

Soviet Union: a large nation in eastern Europe and northern Asia that consisted of 15 member-republics. It existed from 1922 to 1991.

steppe: a level, grass-covered, generally treeless plain that extends in a broad belt over southern parts of European Russia and southwestern Siberia.

taiga: the subarctic evergreen forests of Siberia that are bordered on the north by the treeless tundra and on the south by the grassy steppes.

Trans-Siberian railway: a railroad line that crosses Siberia. There once was a single line—the Trans-Siberian Railroad—that connected Ekaterinburg and Chelyabinsk. No official railroad currently holds this name. The Trans-Siberian Express makes a more than 5,000-mile trip from Moscow to Vladivostok in seven days, using the track of the old Trans-Siberian Railroad during part of the journey.